ir

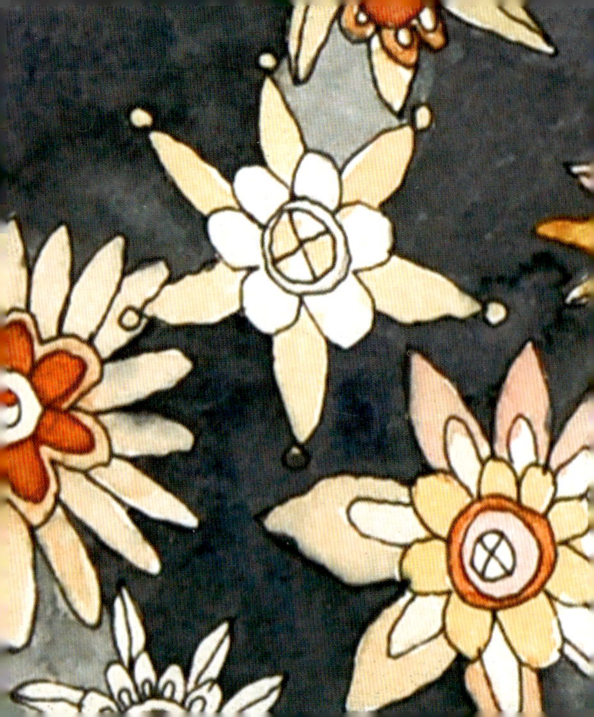

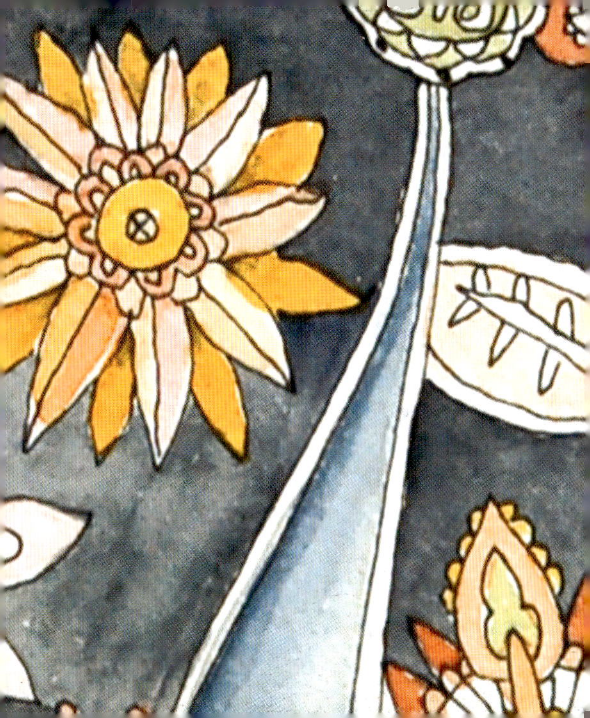

Affirmations
PUBLISHING HOUSE

living words

First published in 2008
Copyright © MMVIII Affirmations Publishing House Pty Ltd

All rights reserved

Published by
Affirmations Publishing House Pty Ltd
34 Hyde Street, Bellingen NSW 2454 Australia
t: +61 2 6655 2350
e: sales@affirmations.com.au
www.affirmations.com.au

Selection and design by Suzanne and Barbara Maher
Illustrations © Cate Edwards 2008
Edited by Suzanne and Barbara Maher

10 9 8 7 6 5 4

ISBN 978-0-9804060-5-4

Printed in China on recycled paper using vegetable based inks.

A little book of

inspiration

Selection and design by
Suzanne and Barbara Maher
with illustrations by Cate Edwards

What lies behind us
and what lies before us
are tiny matters
compared to what lies
within us.
RALPH WALDO EMERSON

No matter what,
your path is yours.
Devote every moment
of your life to improving
your dreams.
Love your world.

From a little spark
may burst a mighty flame.

DANTE

The greatest thing
anyone can do in this world
is to make the most possible
out of the stuff that has been given to them.
This is success, and there is no other.

ORISON SWETT MARDEN

We lift ourselves by our thought.
We climb upon
our vision of ourselves.
If you want to enlarge your life,
you must first enlarge
your thought of it and of yourself.
Hold the ideal
of yourself as you long to be,
always, everywhere.

ORISON SWETT MARDEN

Moderation is a fatal thing.
Nothing succeeds like excess.
OSCAR WILDE

If at first you don't succeed,
try something harder.
PROVERB

Mistakes are stepping stones
to success.

To laugh often and much;
to win the respect
of intelligent people
and the affection of children;
to leave the world a better place;
to know even one life
has breathed easier
because you have lived.
This is to have succeeded.

RALPH WALDO EMERSON

Success comes in cans;
not cannots.

Go confidently
in the direction of your dreams.
Live the life you've imagined.

HENRY DAVID THOREAU

Little by little, one walks far.

PERUVIAN PROVERB

There is only one thing for us to do,
and that is to do our level best
right where we are
every day of our lives.
To use our best judgement,
and then to trust the rest
to that Power
which holds the forces
of the universe
in their hands.

ORISON SWETT MARDEN

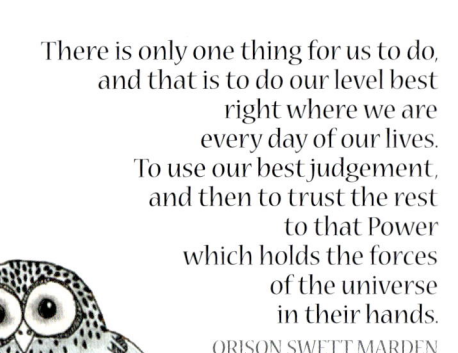

A will
finds a way.

Yesterday is but a dream,
tomorrow but a vision.
But today well lived
makes every yesterday
a dream of happiness,
and every tomorrow a vision of hope.

SANSKRIT PROVERB

For I dipped into the future,
far as the human eye could see,
saw the vision of the world,
and all the wonder that would be.

ALFRED LORD TENNYSON

The only lifelong, reliable motivations
are those that come from within,
and one of the strongest of those
is the joy and pride
that grow from knowing
that you've just done something
as well as you can do it.

LLOYD DOBENS

No one fails who does their best.

ORISON SWETT MARDEN

Far and away
the best prize that life offers
is the chance to work hard
at work worth doing.
THEODORE ROOSEVELT

There is no one quite like you.

It is never too late
to be what you might have been.
GEORGE ELIOT

Success is to be measured
not so much by the position
that you reach in life,
as by the obstacles that you overcome
while trying to succeed.

BROOKER T WASHINGTON

The vision that you hold in your mind,
the ideal that you enthrone in your heart,
this you will build your life by,
and this you will become.

Our thoughts and imagination
are the only real limits
to our possibilities.

There are powers
inside of you which,
if you could discover and use,
would make of you
everything you ever dreamed
or imagined you could become.

ORISON SWETT MARDEN

Do common things
uncommonly well.

The golden opportunity
you are seeking is in yourself.
It is not in your environment,
it is not in luck or chance,
or the help of others;
it is in yourself alone.

MARDEN

If a man does not keep pace
with his companions,
perhaps it is because
he hears a different drummer.

HENRY DAVID THOREAU

To succeed in life,
you need two things:
ignorance
and confidence.

MARK TWAIN

Success is not measured
by what you accomplish,
but by the opposition you have encountered,
and the courage with which
you have maintained the struggle
against overwhelming odds.

MARDEN

It is possible to move a mountain
by carrying away small stones.
CHINESE PROVERB

The greatest achievement
of the human spirit
is to live up to one's opportunities
and to make the most of one's resources.
VAUVENARGUES

Nurture your mind with
great thoughts.
BENJAMIN DISRAELI

Have the simplest of tastes.
Always be satisfied with the best.
OSCAR WILDE

We may run, walk, stumble, drive or fly,
but let us never lose sight
of the reason for the journey.

We must give more
in order to get more.
It is in the generous giving of ourselves
that produces the generous harvest.

ORISON SWETT MARDEN

Do not follow where the path may lead.
Go instead where there is no path,
and leave a trail.

Vision is the art of
seeing the invisible.
JONATHAN SWIFT

Trust in what you love,
continue to do it,
and it will take you
where you need to go.

Don't wait for
extraordinary opportunities.
Seize common occasions
and make them great.
ORISON SWETT MARDEN

May your dreams take you
to the corners of your smiles,
to the highest of your hopes,
to the windows of your opportunities,
and to the most special places
your heart has ever known.

If you keep believing,
the dream that you wish will come true.

How good is life!
ROBERT BROWNING

Hear blessings
dropping their blossoms around you.
RUMI

Find the best in others.
RALPH WALDO EMERSON

Nothing is too good to be true.

Success
is the child of perseverance.
It cannot be coaxed or bribed;
pay the price
and it is yours.

ORISON SWETT MARDEN

If we go down
deep inside ourselves
we find that we possess
exactly what we desire.

SIMONE WEIL

Twenty years from now
you will be more disappointed
by the things you didn't do
than by the ones you did.
So throw off the bowlines.
Sail away from the safe harbour.
Catch the trade winds in your sails.
Explore. Dream.
Discover.

MARK TWAIN

Titles in this series:

A Little Book of Comfort
ISBN 978-0-9757703-2-0

A Little Book of Friends
ISBN 978-0-9757703-3-7

A Little Book of Happiness
ISBN 978-0-9757703-4-4

A Little Book of Inspiration
ISBN 978-0-9804060-5-4

A Little Book of Joy
ISBN 978-0-9804060-4-7

A Little Book of Love
ISBN 978-0-9757703-5-1

Whilst every effort has been made
to acknowledge the author of the quotations used,
please contact the publisher if this has not occurred.

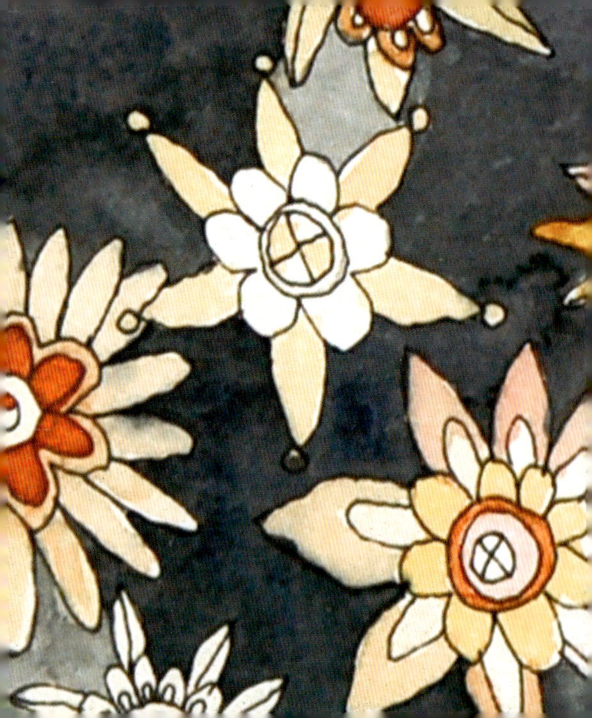

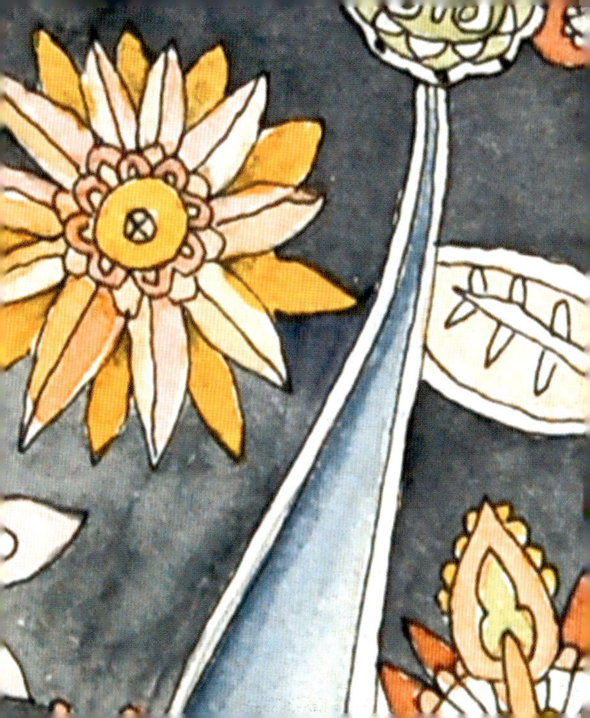

This little book contains a unique collection
of carefully chosen quotations
designed to offer reflection
on the many seasons of our lives.

All Affirmations products are designed
to inspire, uplift and enlighten.
We believe, by passing inspirational messages
from one person to another,
it is helping to create a positive shift
in values on this planet,
thus making a better world for us all.

Affirmations Publishing House Pty Ltd
Bellingen NSW Australia
www.affirmations.com.au   Tel: +61 2 6655 2350